COVER & FRONTISPIECE
Canaletto, Venice: the Bacino di S. Marco
on Ascension Day, c1733–34 (details; **17**)

# A King's Purchase

## King George III and the Collection of Consul Smith

*The Queen's Gallery, Buckingham Palace*

# Contents

FACING PAGE
Canaletto,
London: view from
Somerset House
to the City, c1750
(detail; 14)

Canaletto, London: view from Somerset House to the City, c1750 (**14**)

Canaletto, London: view from Somerset House to Westminster, c1750 (**20**)

# Preface

This booklet accompanies the exhibition of works of art from Smith's collection on view at The Queen's Gallery from March to December 1993. As the drawings had been the subject of an extensive publication (by the foremost Smith scholar, Frances Vivian) and the majority of the paintings had also been included in recent Royal Collection catalogues (by Michael Levey, John Shearman and Christopher White), it was decided that it would be superfluous to produce full entries of the type customarily prepared for the catalogues to exhibitions at The Queen's Gallery. The numbers (in bold) in the captions and text refer to the checklist of exhibits at the back of the booklet (pages 65–70).

The following text is necessarily dependent on each of the above authorities, on the work of Antony Griffiths, Francis Haskell, Oliver Millar, Stuart L. Morrison, Kirsten Aschengreen Piacenti, and on the monographic studies of Anthony Blunt, Ruth Bromberg, W. G. Constable, Edward Croft-Murray, J. G. Links, Karl Parker and Terisio Pignatti. Much assistance has been provided by members of the Royal Collection Department, and by Pippa Mason who has contributed the section concerning Smith's picture frames. Help has also been gratefully received from Alessandro Bettagno, Clarenza Catullo and Paolo Viti, and from Vittorio Guillion Mangilli.

All colour illustrations, and most of the black and white plates, reproduce items in the Royal Collection, which are reproduced by gracious permission of Her Majesty The Queen. Comparative illustrations on pages 18, 25, 28, 39, 42, 50, 52 and 64 are reproduced, respectively, by permission of the Trustees of the British Museum; the Fondazione Giorgio Cini, Istituto di Storia dell'Arte, Venice; the Yale Center for British Art (Paul Mellon Collection), New Haven; the Department of Printing and Graphic Arts, the Houghton Library, Harvard University; the Trustees of the National Gallery, London; the Trustees of the British Library (pages 50 and 52); and Mr Andrew Robison.

# The life of Joseph Smith

## c1674–1770

We do not know precisely when Smith was born, nor where, nor what he looked like. But according to his death certificate of November 1770, he lived to be 96 years old. The armorial bearings which he applied to his books and pictures, and which appear on his gravestone, relate to the Smith family of Essex and Suffolk.

In around 1700, after attending Westminster School, Smith moved to Venice to work with Thomas Williams, a merchant banker of international reputation. When Williams retired twenty years later, Smith took over as manager of the business. As well as banking, the firm was involved in import and export and was used by many British visitors to Venice. Already in 1709 Williams & Smith were assisting Lord Raby in the purchase of works of art. By the time of Williams' departure Smith was acting as agent for several English collectors in the purchase of manuscripts and books, and had entered the Venetian art world. Joseph Smith continued his trading activities until the last years of his life, never moving far from Venice and the Veneto and never returning to England. His brother John was active in London in a similar capacity. John's obituary notice (in 1737) described him as 'Italian merchant'. The two brothers may also have been involved in publishing in London.

British interests in the Venetian Republic were served by both a Resident (or Ambassador) and a Consul. Smith made several attempts to be appointed Resident in Venice, but had to be content with the Consulship, a position which was traditionally given to a merchant banker and which Smith occupied from 1744 to 1760 and again briefly in 1766.

His home was a small palace on the Grand Canal, near the church of SS. Apostoli to the north of the Rialto Bridge. It was leased from the Balbi family, first by Smith's partner, Thomas Williams, and then by Smith himself until in 1740 he purchased the freehold. During the following decade the palace was largely rebuilt (see illustrations on p.39). The inventory made after Smith's death mentions furniture, silverware and porcelain from England. But the remaining contents consisted of paintings, porcelain, books and other treasures acquired and produced mainly in Italy. In 1731 Smith had also purchased the freehold of a small estate at Mogliano, on the road to Treviso on the Venetian mainland. His architect, Visentini, was once again employed to rebuild and improve the house, which Visentini himself recorded in a series of views. The Consul visited Mogliano at weekends and entertained many of his fellow countrymen there, such as Boswell and Robert Adam. The villa was sold to the Spanish Ambassador in Venice shortly before Smith's death. No trace of it has survived.

FACING PAGE
Canaletto,
London: view from
Somerset House
to Westminster, c1750
(detail; **20**)

Smith had a serious and informed interest in architecture, and in particular the work of Andrea Palladio, of whom he believed (wrongly, it now appears) that he owned a portrait. His publishing house, the Pasquali Press, brought out a number of architectural volumes in the 1730s and 1740s. Among the books described as being in preparation in 1761 was the fine facsimile edition of Palladio's *Architettura* of 1570.

Smith was twice married, firstly (c1717) to an English opera singer Catherine Tofts, the mother of a short-lived only child, John (1721–7). Catherine died in 1755 and two years later the Consul married Elizabeth Murray, sister of the British Resident. By now Smith was over eighty and his financial affairs were in a decline, owing largely to the disturbances to European trade caused by the wars of the 1740s and 1750s. In 1760 he retired from the Consulship and in the following year he made a will, leaving the bulk of his estate to his wife, after small bequests to nephews and nieces, and to English friends. The inheritance consisted chiefly of 'the considerable collections' that he had formed, together with the stock in trade of his business as bookseller and printer (managed by Pasquali). In March 1770 he added a codicil to the will, and eight months later he died, of 'senile fever'. In 1778 Elizabeth Smith moved to England, where she spent the remaining ten years of her life.

FACING PAGE
Canaletto,
Venice: the Piazzetta
towards the
Torre dell'Orologio,
c1727–29 (detail; **22**)

Antonio Visentini,
Smith's villa at Mogliano:
the entrance front,
c1747 (**2**)

# The collection of Joseph Smith

Smith appears to have begun to collect as a direct result of his activity as agent for the purchase of manuscripts, paintings and so on, for his fellow countrymen. He thus became acquainted with several of the leading collectors and artists of the day, and acquired many of their works, by purchase, commission or occasionally by gift.

He was buying manuscripts and books in the 1710s, and paintings (and probably drawings too) by the 1720s. In 1724 he published his first catalogue of incunabula, indicating what appears to have been his first and perhaps greatest interest. A number of commissions for paintings are documented from the 1720s, and particularly the 1740s, the period of the major improvements to both Smith's palace and to his villa. In 1738 John Breval noted the 'many excellent Pieces of Painting, Sculpture, etc.', including the 'admirable' Cignani cartoons in Smith's Venetian home. The purchase of pictures from Pellegrini's estate in 1741 and of paintings and drawings from Sagredo's estate in 1752 added many fine works by earlier masters to the collection. When Robert Adam visited Smith at Mogliano in 1757 he was shown 'as pretty a collection of pictures as I have ever seen'. Smith's somewhat limited network of contacts – chiefly the Venetian domain and the Netherlands: he never visited Rome – resulted in the many *lacunae* in the collection: no classical landscapes (by Poussin, Claude or their followers) and few fine seventeenth-century Italian paintings. Most surprisingly, there was nothing by G. B. Tiepolo. He owned a figure of Neptune by Giambologna, and commissioned a few pieces of sculpture for his garden at Mogliano, but his interest in the ancient world was limited to its literature (his library contained fine illuminated copies of the classics), its coins (of which he made a fine collection) and to views of Rome by Canaletto: he does not appear to have acquired any of the antiquities (or pseudo-antiquities) marketed by his friend Piranesi. Likewise, tapestries, fine furniture and porcelain did not concern him particularly, although he owned a Meissen service decorated with his arms.

In Smith's will of 1761 he wrote that his collections formed 'the Principal Part of my Estate'. The text of the will is an important source of information on the content of these collections. There were cameos and intaglios valued at 7000 ducats (£1,225), and precious jewels and gold coins, all of which were at the time on deposit as surety against a debt of 16,000 ducats (£2,800). Smith wrote that 'I was always desirous that some entire classes of my collection might remain united, such as my Library, Drawings, Gemms or Pictures'. The contents of his library had already been made public, through the appearance of the *Bibliotheca Smithiana* in 1755. The catalogue of the collection of gems – 'the work of 40 years united together' – was noted as being in the press (it was published in 1767), while Smith's large-scale cartoons by Cignani and

Carlo Cignani,
Bacchus and Ariadne,
c1680 (ML 452)

New Testament paintings by Sebastiano Ricci had been described, engraved and published (in 1749) at Smith's expense. As we will see, the surviving lists of the paintings are inadequate on various accounts. However, they suggest a collection of around 500 pictures altogether.

It is difficult to judge how Smith's collection compared with those of his contemporaries, for none of these has survived intact. His friend and fellow-Venetian, Anton Maria Zanetti, had a very comparable collection of both paintings, drawings and engraved gems. Zanetti also owned paintings by Poussin, and himself engraved the works of Tiepolo. But the group of paintings by Canaletto gathered together by Joseph Smith was unequalled.

In 1762 the collection that Smith had described in his will was sold to George III. However, the posthumous inventory of the Venetian palace, and the subsequent sales of Smith's property, demonstrate that he was the owner of a very considerable collection at the time of his death. In July 1770 it was recorded that Smith (now ninety-six years old) 'had been going on in his usual way, of purchasing books, medals, pictures and other curiositys of which the house is full'. The catalogues of the sales (in

which the printed books, engravings and paintings were listed) are sufficiently detailed to demonstrate that Smith's 'second' collection was almost as large – and at least as interesting – as that disposed of in 1762. Nearly two thousand lots of printed books were offered at auction in London in January 1773. Three years later Christie's held two separate sales devoted to Smith's art collection: a six-day sale (containing 490 lots in all) of prints and drawings and a two-day sale (comprising 203 lots) of paintings and sculpture. A further 16 lots of plate and jewels were sold in 1789 after Mrs Smith's death. However, these sale catalogues were also the means whereby Smith's later collection was dispersed, and it is only through an extraordinary – as yet largely unattempted – process of reconstruction that we can form a true impression of the objects with which Smith was surrounded at the time of his death.

ABOVE
Canaletto,
Venice: the Grand Canal
from the Carità to the
Bacino di S. Marco,
c1730 (detail; **15**)

FACING PAGE
detail

# The King's purchase

At the time of the conclusion of the purchase of Smith's collection King George III was not yet twenty-five. His father, Frederick, Prince of Wales, had died in 1751, having formed a considerable collection of paintings and drawings. By any standards, but particularly in comparison with George I and George II, Frederick was a notable patron of the arts. His flare and interest were inherited by his son and heir.

In the mid-1750s the young George, Prince of Wales, was active in the purchase of books – particularly botanical works – at London sales. His chief adviser, the Earl of Bute, was himself a passionate bibliophile. It is therefore very likely that the abortive negotiations for the purchase of Smith's library, mentioned in his will of 1761, had involved the future George III. The 'treaty . . . commenced on the Part of a Royal Purchaser', concerned Smith's 'Library, according to the printed Catalogue, made public', which was to be purchased at 20,000 sequins, i.e. £10,000. Discussions had been terminated because of the Seven Years War (1756–63), which also brought about a worsening of Smith's own financial situation.

James Adam reported that by 1760 Smith was 'devilishly poor' but so 'eaten up with' vanity that he doubted he would ever bring himself to sell his collection. However, when writing his will (in April 1761) Smith knew that his widow would have to raise funds 'to establish thereby a decent and comfortable settlement for the remainder of her life'. In the event it was Smith rather than his wife who concluded the sale, just over a year later. In October 1760 the young prince had ascended the throne as King George III. Negotiations for the purchase – of Smith's whole collection – were handled, on behalf of the King, by Bute's brother, James Stuart Mackenzie (British Envoy to Turin 1758–61). In July 1762 Mackenzie informed Smith that the King 'has been pleased to think the Collection not to be unworthy of his possession' and the figure of £20,000 was agreed.

The following winter Mackenzie and the Royal Librarian, Richard Dalton, visited Venice to oversee the final details of the sale and transfer. In December 1762 London newspapers reported that the purchase of the collection would 'make the finest Collection in Europe; . . . Tickets will be given to the Nobility and Gentry to admit them to see it'. In January 1763 Dalton (still in Venice) inscribed and signed two copies of the *Bibliotheca* to the effect that the contents were 'all in perfect good order'. One of the copies has valuations (in ducats) noted in the margin. In February 1763 the cases containing the collection were awaited at Livorno, for onward shipment to London. They appear to have travelled with the other great collection of drawings purchased by George III in Italy, that of Cardinal Albani.

*Rembrandt pinxit, oli p.t. lat vne x, Exãt Venetiis in demo J. SMITH.*       *J.B.Jackson figuras juxta Archetypum Sculp.&excudit.1738*

Acceperunt ergo Corpus JESU, & ligaverunt illud linteis
cum Aromatibus, ficut mos eft Judæis fepelire. *S.Joan.Cap.XIX.Ver.XL.*

*Perilluſtri ac Præclaro     Viro D. JOSEPHO SMITH
Inſigne hoc Opus affabre    in Ligno cœlavit,& in sui
obſequii & grati Animi monu-   mentum humiliter devovet
                                              J.B.Jackson*

Among the pictures that belonged to Smith but became detached from his collection in the late eighteenth century was Rembrandt's *Descent from the Cross* (now in the National Gallery), seen here in J. B. Jackson's woodcut of 1738 dedicated to Smith. It was included in the posthumous sale of the collection of Richard Dalton, the King's Librarian and Surveyor of Pictures, in 1791.

Apart from the *Bibliotheca Smithiana* (in which all the books, manuscripts, engravings and most of the drawings are listed) no proper inventories have survived relating to the items involved in the sale. Although (as we will see) there are a large number of clues to associate particular oil paintings with the Smith collection, the first picture lists date from some years after the purchase. The circumstances in which a number of the pictures included in these lists became separated from those which remain in the Royal Collection today – and were sold in London in the 1780s and 1790s with pictures from the collections of Joshua Reynolds and Richard Dalton – will probably never be clarified. Important paintings such as Rembrandt's *Descent from the Cross* and Bellini's *Agony in the Garden*, both now in the National Gallery, London, thus left the Smith corpus.

# Paintings and Drawings

Joseph Smith was well known to many of the foremost Venetian artists of the day and his collection of paintings and drawings reflected this fact very clearly. He handled some of their finest works, acting both as agent and supporter, as publicist and as private collector.

Catherine Tofts, Smith's first wife, was a member of the operatic and theatrical world in which Marco and Sebastiano Ricci also worked, as stage designers. Whether Smith met Catherine through the Ricci, or the Ricci through Catherine, is not known, but Smith's first contact with Marco and Sebastiano dates from around the time of his marriage, in 1717. Most of Sebastiano Ricci's finest works of the 1720s were purchased by Smith, who considered Sebastiano the leading painter of the time. Smith was also acquainted with Rosalba Carriera and with Antonio Visentini before 1720; Visentini acted as illustrator, engraver, architect and general artistic factotum to Smith throughout the remainder of the latter's life. Canaletto, born in 1697, and Zuccarelli, born in 1702, were several years younger than these artists and therefore encountered Smith rather later: Canaletto in the mid-1720s and Zuccarelli soon after his arrival in Venice c1730.

Works by Rosalba, Zuccarelli and Canaletto were supplied to Smith's English clients, and other paintings and drawings by these artists entered his own collection at the same time. By 1728 Smith was also commissioning large-scale paintings from Canaletto. Two sets of over-door 'capricci' were ordered (from Canaletto, and from Visentini and Zuccarelli) in the 1740s as part of a fresh wave of commissions – perhaps to mark Smith's new status as Consul.

The process of forming or adding to the collection is mainly undocumented and the origin of the majority of older paintings owned by Smith is therefore unknown. Likewise, the detailed list of pictures mentioned in Smith's will does not appear to have survived. The content of the collection sold by him to the King therefore has to be reconstructed from the information included in reproductive engravings, from the evidence of the semi-uniform frames (in which most of his pictures appear to have been placed: see below, p.64) and from two early nineteenth-century inventories of pictures in the Royal Collection, known as the Italian and the Flemish and Dutch Lists (which included 351 and 149 paintings respectively). These appear to be copies of lost originals, which may have accompanied Smith's paintings at the time of their purchase. The Italian List is headed 'Catalogue of Paintings of the Italian School all in fine preservation, and in carved gilt frames in modern and elegant taste. Bought by His Majesty in Italy, and now chiefly at Kew'. It included 54 paintings by Canaletto, 36 by Zuccarelli, 34 by Marco Ricci, 28 by Sebastiano Ricci and 24 by Rosalba. A total of 219 works by eighteenth-century Italian artists were listed, of which 162 are still recognisable in the collection. Of the remaining 130 or so paintings by earlier Italian masters, under half can be located today. The problem of misattribution is considerable, particularly with the Flemish and Dutch List, only a quarter of which have been linked to pictures in the present Royal Collection.

The drawings acquired by George III from Smith were all mounted in albums – apart from the framed pastels and chalk drawings by Rosalba and Piazzetta. The individual volumes (containing drawings by Canaletto, Figino, Marco and Sebastiano Ricci and Visentini) were listed alongside the books in the *Bibliotheca Smithiana*. A brief description of the contents of each volume was supplied in independent manuscript notes in Smith's hand and valuations for the more important volumes were added to one of the 'file copies' of the *Bibliotheca* (now in the British Library). Although the *Bibliotheca Smithiana* was published in 1755, the text had been prepared several years earlier so the drawings from the Sagredo collection (purchased in 1752) were not included. All these volumes are identifiable in the inventory of the King's drawings made c1800, and their contents – now mostly removed from the albums and mounted independently – remain in the Royal Collection.

The apparently haphazard process of acquisition led to a collection of very uneven quality: numerous high points, but – particularly for the older pictures – several copies or studio works. As such it was probably fairly typical of its time. The collection that Smith sold to George III was chiefly remarkable for its Venetian eighteenth-century works (particularly by Canaletto), its manuscripts and its incunables; and it is also remarkable because – alone among the collections formed in Venice in the early eighteenth century – it has remained largely intact.

FACING PAGE
Canaletto, Rome: the Arch of Septimius Severus, 1742 (detail; 13)

# Sebastiano Ricci

Sebastiano Ricci (1659–1734) was the oldest of the contemporary Venetian masters befriended by Smith, who considered him the leading artist of the time. Sebastiano was born in the mountain town of Belluno and trained in Venice, but thereafter worked chiefly in Bologna, Turin, Parma, Rome and Florence before returning to Venice in 1708. Between 1711 and 1716 Sebastiano (with his nephew, Marco) was chiefly active in London, working for various private patrons as well as designing for the theatre and opera houses. Soon after returning to Venice, Sebastiano produced the series of seven large paintings of New Testament subjects which are first recorded in Smith's collection (in 1742) and may have been painted for him. An early commentator states that Marco Ricci painted the backgrounds in the series. During the 1720s the Ricci were engaged by the theatrical impresario, Owen McSwiney, to paint a series of allegorical paintings commemorating the great men of recent English history.

The circumstances of Smith's acquisitions of the many paintings by Sebastiano recorded in his collection are not known. It is likely that they were purchased from the artist

Sebastiano Ricci, Two heads for The Adoration, 1726 (**61**)

FACING PAGE
Sebastiano Ricci, The Adoration of the Magi, 1726 (detail; **24**)

Sebastiano Ricci, The Holy Family with Saints Elizabeth and John the Baptist, c1710 (30)

direct before the latter's death in 1734. The Italian List records twenty-eight paintings by Sebastiano and eight collaborative works by Sebastiano and Marco. Eighteen paintings by Sebastiano and six joint works have survived in the Royal Collection.

Sebastiano's style looks back to that of Veronese, as well as pointing forward – in its lightness of touch – to that of G. B. Tiepolo. His painting of *The Finding of Moses*, which may have been commissioned by Smith, appears to have entered the Royal Collection (from Smith) with an attribution to Veronese.

Smith's drawings by Sebastiano Ricci are still mostly contained in the album in which he placed them. This was noted in the *Bibliotheca Smithiana* as 'Sebastiano Ricci, *Monochromata & Experimenta*', and was valued at 1,200 ducats (£210). The album is carefully made up, beginning

with an engraving of the artist's self-portrait, followed by two illuminated pages by Visentini. The second of these is inscribed 'Sebastiani Ricci Bellunensis, huiusce seculi pictoris facile principis opus'. The 211 drawings were pasted on to sheets of thick cream paper, to which parallel framing lines – washed with a variety of different colours – were added. The junction between drawing and mounting sheet was marked by a thick gold line.

Many of the drawings are preparatory studies for paintings by Sebastiano which also belonged to Smith: variant compositional studies, rapid sketches or detailed life drawings, normally in ink and wash but occasionally in coloured chalks. The earliest of the drawings in Smith's volume dates from c1695 and the latest relates to work of 1730. During the recent remounting operation involving the few drawings that have been removed from the album, Smith's initials 'JS', followed by a number, have been

revealed on the versos. A selection process is presumably indicated, perhaps in the artist's studio.

The fact that the drawings have been enclosed within an album for almost their entire existence has meant that they have been protected from the harmful effects of light and has contributed to their excellent state of preservation. A very similar album of Sebastiano's drawings was made up for Anton Maria Zanetti the Elder and is now in the Venice Accademia.

TOP LEFT
Antonio Visentini, Prefatory page to Smith's volume of drawings by Sebastiano Ricci (BV 532)

TOP RIGHT
Marco Ricci, The artist's uncle, Sebastiano Ricci (EC-M 2)

BOTTOM RIGHT
Anton Maria Zanetti the Elder, Marco Ricci (Istituto di Storia dell'Arte, Fondazione Giorgio Cini, Venice)

# Marco Ricci

Marco Ricci (1676–1730) was the nephew, pupil and collaborator of Sebastiano Ricci, whom he predeceased. His first contacts with England probably took place in 1708, when Marco and G. A. Pellegrini were invited to London by Lord Manchester. There they were engaged on various commissions – which included theatrical work for McSwiney – and met Catherine Tofts, who in 1711 moved to Venice and six years later married Joseph Smith.

After returning to Venice in 1716, Marco resided with his uncle and produced the background elements for many of his paintings. He was also much involved with the theatrical and operatic community, designing scenery and drawing caricatures of many of the singers. The small landscapes or capricci, painted in gouache on leather, were painted at this time. Thirty-three of these were included in the Italian List; thirty-two survive in the Royal Collection to this day. One of them is inscribed in ink on the backboard 'per Madama Smit'. The Italian List also mentions six landscapes, one 'Antique Ruins the last peice of Marco' and two vast canvases over 6ft. high by 9ft. wide, all of which were described as collaborative works by uncle and nephew. Most of these can still be identified in the Royal Collection.

Marco Ricci, Courtyard of a villa, c1728 (112)

FACING PAGE
detail

Marco Ricci, The Rehearsal of an opera, c1709, with the singer Catherine Tofts (Joseph Smith's first wife) in the foreground (detail; Paul Mellon Collection, Yale Center for British Art, New Haven)

Marco Ricci, Italian town caprice, 1719; inscribed on the frame 'per Madama Smit' and probably presented by the artist to Catherine Tofts (who had married Smith in 1717) (**105**)

As with Sebastiano, Smith doubtless obtained his large collection of drawings by Marco Ricci direct from the studio. Two volumes of Marco's drawings were included in the *Bibliotheca Smithiana*: '*Experimenta et Schedae*', valued at 2,200 ducats – precisely the figure given to Smith's albums of drawings by Sebastiano Ricci and by Canaletto – and '*Caricature diverse*', valued at only 500 ducats. The caricature volume has survived largely intact, but the main volume of Marco's drawings appears to have been dismantled soon after entering the Royal Collection. George III's inventory lists one volume of 52 landscape drawings, a second volume of 54 drawings of ruins, scenery, etc., and a portfolio containing 27 large landscape drawings. All these are still in the Royal Collection, in addition to 12 even larger landscape drawings, now badly faded having been framed and exposed to light over many years.

Smith's friend Zanetti owned another volume of caricatures, and a series of 141 landscape drawings by Marco. The drawings from the collections of Smith and Zanetti are crucial as starting points in any study of the very varied styles and techniques of Marco's graphic work. Smith also owned most of Marco's etchings, which are an interesting prelude to the etched work of Canaletto.

Marco Ricci, Hall with staircase, c1726 (**97**)

# Paintings by Canaletto

Joseph Smith owned the finest collection of paintings, drawings and etchings by Antonio Canal, called Canaletto (1697–1768) that has ever been assembled. Fifty of the fifty-four pictures by the artist noted in the Italian List survive in the Royal Collection.

The artist was trained by his father as a theatrical designer but soon turned to view painting. By 1725 it was accepted that the elderly Luca Carlevarijs had been supplanted by Canaletto, whose views of Venice were already being eagerly sought. The artist's chief customers were foreigners: like Marco and Sebastiano Ricci, he was involved in McSwiney's allegorical tombs series from the early 1720s. The 2nd Duke of Richmond was closely connected with this scheme and in 1727 received two Venetian views by Canaletto, painted on copper: these were despatched by McSwiney and were delivered to the Duke by John Smith, Joseph's brother. But Canaletto's dealings with his patrons were complicated by what they saw as his unreasonable behaviour – he overcharged and took on too much work. Smith, who was a business associate of McSwiney, therefore acted as the artist's middle man, ensuring that commissions were completed on time, for an agreed sum, and seeing to matters such as transportation and framing

The close relationship between Smith and Canaletto is largely undocumented. It appears to have commenced in the later 1720s, the approximate date of the six large views (four upright and two oblong) of the Piazza and Piazzetta di S. Marco in his collection. These pictures, generally considered to be among Canaletto's finest works, may originally have been set into the panelling of a room, possibly in Smith's palace in Venice. By 1730 Smith was corresponding with Samuel Hill concerning two paintings by Canaletto. Hill's nephew (and heir), Samuel Egerton, was apprenticed to Smith in Venice. Other paintings by Canaletto were acquired – through Smith – at this time by members of the Howard, Leeds and Essex families. The series of twenty-two small and two large canvasses by Canaletto, now at Woburn Abbey, were purchased with the assistance of Smith in the mid-1730s.

By 1730 Smith claimed that work was nearly complete on the series of engravings after Canaletto's views of Venice, issued in 1735 as the *Prospectus Magni Canalis Venetiarum*. The fourteen relevant paintings were all owned by Smith and are today in the Royal Collection. The *Prospectus* served as a fine advertisement for Canalet-to's work and for Smith's services as agent. A second edition was issued in 1742. This contained twenty-four further plates. But whereas the original fourteen views remained with Smith, only one of the additional views belonged to him: three had been acquired by the Duke of Bedford, three by the Duke of Leeds, two by Earl Fitzwilliam, and eight were part of an important group of Canaletto's paintings known as the Harvey series.

The outbreak of the War of the Austrian Succession in 1740 disrupted the flow of foreign tourists to Venice, and Canaletto (or possibly Smith) now decided to develop new subjects for his pictures. A journey up the Brenta Canal resulted in a number of paintings and drawings and a remarkable group of etchings. In 1742 Canaletto signed and dated five large upright canvases representing the chief ancient sites of Rome. Like the earlier upright series (of Venice), these belonged to Smith – and then to George III – and may have been intended for another room in his Venetian palace. The choice of subject-matter is on one level entirely natural for an Englishman in Italy in the mid-eighteenth century, but on another level somewhat surprising: Smith is not documented as having visited Rome, and Canaletto's early biographers record only one visit to that city, in 1719. The details in the Roman views may depend on records made at that time, together with prints or drawings by others of the relevant monuments.

By now Canaletto had very few patrons other than Smith. The Consul's next commission was for a set of thirteen large oblong overdoors, incorporating idealised Palladian elements in Venetian settings. Nine of the paintings, datable 1743/4, remain in the Royal Collection. Realising that England provided the chief market for his work, Canaletto now transferred his activities to London where he is first recorded in May 1746. He travelled with a letter from Smith to McSwiney, asking for an introduction to the Duke of Richmond. While in England (intermittently between 1746 and 1755) he worked for the Dukes of Richmond and Beaufort, the future Duke of Northumberland and the Earl of Warwick, providing fine topographical records of different parts of the country. Canaletto's luggage on his return to Venice must have

FACING PAGE
Canaletto, Venice: Piazza S. Marco with the south-west corner of the Basilica, c1727–29 (detail; **26**)

Engraving by Visentini of Piazzetta's portrait of Canaletto and of his own self-portrait
(from *Prospectus Magni Canalis Venetiarum*, 1735)

included many other English subjects (painted or drawn), for Smith obtained a number of London views which would have served as nostalgic mementoes of his earliest years. But thereafter very few works by Canaletto were acquired by Smith.

During Canaletto's stay in England it was noted that 'he dos not produce works so well done as those in [i.e. of] Venice . . . which were in Collections here'. From the mid-1740s there is indeed a noticeable change in his style; his later paintings lack the brilliance and bravura of his earlier Venetian views and his work thus became easier to imitate.

In view of the close association between Canaletto and Smith throughout the majority of the artist's working life, it would be natural to expect that Canaletto had a passing knowledge of the other paintings in Smith's collection. The similarity in his handling of paint to that in Vermeer's *Lady at the Virginals* has often been remarked upon. So too has the possible influence of the Neeffs interiors of Antwerp cathedral on Canaletto's interiors of S. Marco. We may assume that the many fine illustrated books in Smith's library would also have been available to Canaletto, to provide details of Palladian designs or Roman edifices to assist him in his work.

FACING PAGE
Canaletto, Venice: Piazza S. Marco with the south-west corner of the Basilica, c1727 (detail; **54**)

FACING PAGE
Canaletto, Venice:
the interior of S. Marco
by day, c1755 (42)

Canaletto, Venice:
the interior of S. Marco
by night (?), c1725 (41)

35

# Drawings and etchings by Canaletto

Smith's collection of drawings by Canaletto was complimentary to that of his paintings. The studies were mostly kept by Smith in a volume containing 100 folios, in addition to a frontispiece by Visentini. This was listed in the *Bibliotheca Smithiana* as 'Canaletto, *Experimenta et Schedae*' and was given the same valuation as the Sebastiano Ricci volume (2,200 ducats). Smith noted the contents of the volume as 139 drawings, 21 etchings and 2 engravings reproducing London views. He also observed that among the drawings were some relating to his own pictures, located in his houses in Venice and Mogliano. But few – if any – of Smith's drawings by Canaletto can properly be described as preparatory studies of the type that would have been made on the spot. Instead they are mostly either records of the proposed finished appearance of a picture, or works of art in their own right.

Three other drawings by Canaletto were kept by Smith at the back of his volume of Visentini's prints and drawings. A total of 143 drawings by Canaletto remain in the Royal Collection. The majority of these were produced in the 1730s. By the end of that decade the artist had begun to experiment with the use of wash – instead of hatching – to produce tonal variations. The drawings associated with the journey along the Brenta, from the early 1740s, have an informality which leads naturally on to the *Vedute Ideate*.

Canaletto finally returned from England in 1755 with a choice group of London views which soon entered the Consul's collection. Very few later purchases were made by Smith. The last of Canaletto's drawings to be acquired by Smith was probably the great virtuoso capriccio, illustrated opposite, a veritable *tour de force* of perspectival draughtsmanship executed c1760.

Canaletto's thirty-one known etchings probably all date from the late 1730s and early 1740s. Many earlier Venetian view painters (for instance, Carlevarijs, Marco Ricci and Marieschi) had produced etchings, and the informality of the medium evidently appealed to Canaletto too. The possible inter-relationship between Canaletto and Smith's friend Piranesi, who was born in Mogliano in 1720 and returned (from Rome) to Venice in 1744, is an intriguing one. Most of Canaletto's etchings were issued as a series, including a title page dedicated to Joseph Smith, British Consul, and therefore datable after June 1744. Somewhat surprisingly, the finest series of these etchings belonged not to Smith but to his friend Zanetti and is now in Berlin. However, the set of 46 etchings now at Windsor is still contained in a George III binding and includes many first states, and 15 rare or unique prints. The provenance of the 25 etchings not contained in Smith's Canaletto volume is unknown.

LEFT
Canaletto, Capriccio with terrace and loggia, c1760 (**47**)

FACING PAGE
detail

36

# Visentini and Zuccarelli

Antonio Visentini (1688–1782) trained as a painter under G. A. Pellegrini, but was later active as an architect, engraver, topographer and illustrator, and proved an indispensable artistic factotum to Joseph Smith. The first record of Smith's association with Visentini occurs in 1717. The Consul was certainly behind Visentini's commission to engrave Canaletto's views of the Grand Canal (first published as the *Prospectus* in 1735), and his employment as chief illustrator to the Pasquali Press. Visentini also designed and engraved Smith's bookplate, and doubtless also the dye-stamp bearing his Arms which appears on so many of his books. The fine title pages at the front of each of Smith's albums of drawings were also Visentini's responsibility. In addition, Smith employed Visentini as architect at the villa at Mogliano (from 1731) and for alterations to his Venetian palace (from 1740). Visentini also made numerous architectural survey drawings of Venetian buildings. Many of these were drawn for Smith. The *Bibliotheca Smithiana* notes three volumes of architectural studies, together with an album of designs and prints by Visentini, including the series of monochrome views of the villa at Mogliano.

Like Smith, Visentini was greatly interested in the designs and theories of the sixteenth-century Venetian architect, Palladio, whose work they considered infinitely superior to that of the Baroque architects. In collaboration with Francesco Zuccarelli (1702–88), Visentini painted a series of eleven overdoor capricci for Smith, featuring English Neo-Palladian buildings (copied by Visentini from publications by Colen Campbell and William Kent) in landscape settings by Zuccarelli.

Zuccarelli was the youngest of the artists employed by Smith, who was an important influence on his career. The artist arrived in Venice from Florence c1730, and by the end of that decade his landscape paintings were reaching England – possibly via Smith. All of the Consul's own paintings by Zuccarelli appear to date from the 1730s and 1740s. In 1752 the artist visited England for the first time and in the following year Orlandi's *Abecedario Pittorico* named Smith as the key figure in deciding Zuccarelli's future career. From the 1750s he worked almost exclusively in England, and Smith appears to have acquired none of his later works. Zuccarelli was a founder member of the Royal Academy (1768), and in 1771 was paid for two paintings commissioned by the King. Twenty-seven

Francesco Zuccarelli, Landscape with Diana and the chase, c1740 (**109**)

paintings by Zuccarelli, together with eight works of collaboration with Visentini (the overdoors mentioned above) survive in the Royal Collection.

FACING PAGE
Smith's Venetian home (the Palazzo Balbi, now Mangilli-Valmarana) on the Grand Canal. The original gothic façade was shown in Visentini's engraving (after Canaletto's painting) in the *Prospectus* (1735; lower left, detail).
Upper left is Visentini's drawing of the new façade, completed (to his designs) in 1751 (Houghton Library, Harvard University) Lower right is a detail from Canaletto's painting of the Grand Canal to the north of the Rialto (**19**) in which the new façade was painted over the original gothic front – presumably on Smith's orders, in the 1750s.
Upper right is the present façade of the Palazzo.

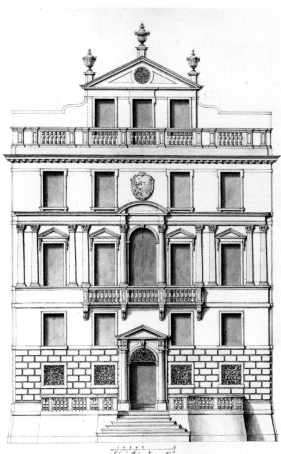

Facciata del Palazzo Smit, Console di sua Maestà Britanica, in Venetia sopra il Canal Grande.

Rosalba Carriera, Self-portrait, c1745 (**104**)

# Rosalba Carriera and Piazzetta

Rosalba Carriera (1675–1757) may have been the first artist to be befriended by Smith. She was Venetian by birth but was active in many different European centres. Smith appears to have met Rosalba before 1720, possibly through his lawyer Carlo Gabrieli, who was the artist's godfather. By this time Rosalba already had various contacts in the British Isles, which she established (and maintained) independently of Smith. The Italian List includes 38 works by Rosalba: portraits, historical and religious pieces, in miniature and in pastel. This may have been the largest collection of her work ever formed. Rosalba's self-portrait in old age (illustrated opposite) was given to Smith by Rosalba, and was engraved in his collection soon after. Only five works by Rosalba have survived in the Royal Collection.

Giovanni Battista Piazzetta (1683–1754) was rather younger than Rosalba, but predeceased her. The Italian List mentions seven religious paintings by Piazzetta, but the only works by the artist in the Royal Collection today are the 36 drawings in black chalk, the 'têtes de caractères'. Piazzetta's reputation for this type of subject was already established by 1720. The artist is not known to have been closely associated with Smith, but his activity as a dealer, artistic agent, painter and illustrator would have ensured that their paths crossed. The image of Canaletto engraved by Visentini for the *Prospectus* was based on Piazzetta's original portrait (now lost). Although the series of heads by Piazzetta now at Windsor – in black and white chalk, on paper which has faded from blue to grey-brown – is not documented in either Smith's or George III's collections, the drawings were almost certainly acquired from Smith. Unlike his other drawings, they were probably framed up at the time of their acquisition.

Giovanni Battista Piazzetta, Self-portrait, c1730 (**103**)

# Earlier Italian Masters

Although the chief strengths of Smith's collection lay in the works of his contemporaries, around a quarter of his paintings were by Italian artists of the fifteenth, sixteenth and seventeenth centuries. Some of these may have been acquired at the sale of the collection of the last Duke of Mantua, which took place in Venice in the 1710s in a building immediately adjacent to that occupied by Smith. Other pictures (including the Bellini shown opposite) were among the fine group of 25 paintings and several volumes of drawings acquired by Smith from the heirs of Zaccaria Sagredo in 1752. The summary list accompanying that purchase is one of the few documents associated with Smith's acquisitions. The source of the majority of his purchases is unrecorded.

Less than half of the earlier paintings on the Italian List are recognisable today, and the attributions attached to those few have rarely stood the test of time. Of the five paintings on the list ascribed to Veronese, one is by Sebastiano Ricci and two others are the work of Veronese's school. The remaining two are not identifiable. None of the three paintings ascribed to Titian are autograph works.

Among Smith's most prized possessions were eight large-scale cartoons by the seventeenth-century Bolognese artist, Carlo Cignani (1628–1719) which were noted in Smith's collection in 1738. The cartoons, which are still in the Royal Collection, were engraved by Liotard in 1743 and discussed in an essay by P. E. Gherardi published in 1749.

---

FACING PAGE
Giovanni Bellini, Portrait of a young man, c1507 (11)

Giovanni Bellini, The Agony in the Garden, c1465 (National Gallery, London). This picture was noted in the Italian List as the work of Andrea Mantegna, but was included in the sale of Sir Joshua Reynolds's collection in 1795, by which time it had evidently left the Royal Collection

Raphael, Massacre of the Innocents, c1510 (**74**)

The purchase from the heirs of Zaccaria Sagredo in 1752 involved several volumes of Old Master drawings, including three 'collected in the time of the Carracci' which Sagredo had purchased from the Bonfiglioli collection in 1728. As well as works by members of the Carracci family and school, the Bonfiglioli collection included a fine group of drawings by Raphael (1483–1520) and his pupils. Late seventeenth- and early eighteenth-century descriptions assist in the identification of several ex-Bonfiglioli drawings within the present Royal Collection. Whereas some of these drawings were evidently framed up by the Bonfiglioli family, they were kept in albums in Sagredo's and Smith's collections.

The Sagredo purchase also appears to have included the unparalleled series of over 200 drawings (contained within four volumes) by the seventeenth-century Genoese painter, Giovanni Benedetto Castiglione (c1610–63/5). (The Italian List includes eleven paintings by the artist, but none remains in the Collection today.) The presence of these drawings in Venice during the early and middle years of the eighteenth century is clearly reflected in the work of G. B. Tiepolo. Several of the drawings were copied by Fragonard during his stay in Venice in 1760.

But the source of other volumes of drawings in Smith's collection is undocumented. These include Giulio Campi's studies of Trajan's Column and a volume of miscellaneous drawings by G. A. Figino. These two series, together with the drawings by Sebastiano Ricci, Visentini and the caricature album, have remained largely undisturbed at Windsor in the bindings (with ornamented title pages by Visentini) into which Smith placed them around 250 years ago.

In view of his origins, and his continuing contact with England (described by Jonathan Richardson in 1728 as 'le cabinet des dessins' of Europe), it is curious that Smith appears to have acquired no drawings from English collections – with the exception of some architectural studies obtained to assist Visentini.

Giovanni Benedetto Castiglione, Nativity with God the Father, c1655 (**70**)

# Northern masters

It may come as some surprise to learn that Vermeer's painting of *The Lady at the Virginals* was acquired by George III from Consul Smith. It is included in the Dutch and Flemish List as the work of Frans van Mieris, and was described as 'A Woman playing on a Spinnet in presence of a Man seems to be her father'. The picture had formerly belonged to the Venetian artist G. A. Pellegrini, who worked extensively in northern Europe (in the Netherlands, Germany and England). Following Pellegrini's death in 1741, Smith purchased his collection and thus acquired a fine group of northern paintings which included works by Rubens, Post, Neeffs and Molenaer, as well as the Vermeer.

A further work attributed to Mieris was included among the fourteen northern paintings acquired by Smith from Sagredo in 1752. The remainder of the Consul's Netherlandish works – estimated at 150 in all – were probably acquired through his business contacts in Amsterdam and elsewhere. The Dutch and Flemish List includes thirteen pictures attributed to Van Dyck, of which only one is now accepted as by that artist, while another is by Fetti, two are attributed to Coques and others are either unattributed or unlocated. Of the ten supposed Rembrandts, only one (*The Descent from the Cross*, now in the National Gallery) is now thought to be by the master. But – in addition to the above – there are fine paintings from Smith's collection by Berchem, De Heem, Frans Francken II, Steen and Weenix. This part of the collection was entirely typical of the time and place, with a small number of masterpieces and a large proportion of less certain works.

Somewhat surprisingly, Smith does not seem to have imported many works of art from England. An exception was a painting by Wootton (now untraced) included on the Italian List, and a number of items of household furniture noted in the posthumous inventory. Indeed when Madame du Boccage visited Venice in 1757, she noted that Smith's palace was 'entirely in the English taste; the very tables and locks of the gates are made after the manner of that country'.

---

FACING PAGE
Johannes Vermeer, A Lady at the Virginals, 1660–70 (36)

Frans Francken the Younger, A Cabinet, 1617 (35)

Canaletto, The portico with a lantern, c1743 (etching; **59/2**)

# Prints

Joseph Smith occupies an important place in the history of print collecting and print making for he was involved in the creative process as a patron and publisher of engravers, as well as being a keen collector.

Smith's prints, like his drawings, were kept in albums in his library. There they were listed in the *Bibliotheca Smithiana* and there – following the sale to George III in 1762 – replacement and additional volumes of prints were placed during the remaining years of Smith's life. The published catalogue included whole albums devoted to the engraved work of Dürer, the Carracci, Callot and Berchem, each of which received high valuations (660 ducats apiece). Other volumes were devoted to Maratta and Reni, Van Dyck, A. Van Ostade, and many others. The absence of works by the great early Italian print-maker Marcantonio Raimondi from the collection may suggest either that it was chiefly made in the north, or that Marcantonio's works were not widely available in Venice. Like Smith's paintings collection, his print collection was somewhat uneven in its coverage. With the exception of the prints by Smith's contemporaries (Marco Ricci, Canaletto and Visentini), which mostly remain in the Consul's own volumes, the prints from his collection have been disbound and amalgamated with those from other sources. However, it is likely that the majority of the prints sold by Smith to George III remain in the Royal Collection to this day.

In his will (made in 1761) Smith mentioned none of the above-mentioned series. However, he went out of his way to cite Liotard's engravings after works by Sebastiano Ricci and Cignani in his collection, for which Smith stated that he had paid £1,000.

Smith's activity as a patron of the engraver's art probably commenced through his association with Visentini (before 1720) and progressed through his involvement with the Pasquali Press (from c1730). In the 1720s he promoted Canaletto's *Prospectus* (published 1735) and a few years later was the dedicatee of the same artist's series of etched *Vedute*. Apart from Visentini (who engraved Canaletto's paintings) and Liotard, Smith was also closely associated with G. B. Brustolon, P. Monaco, possibly Bartolozzi, and certainly J. B. Jackson, and thus provided vital encouragement to the engraver's, etcher's and wood-cutter's art. Following the sale to George III, Smith formed an important collection of the etchings of his young friend G. B. Piranesi, who was born in Mogliano, close to the site of Smith's country house.

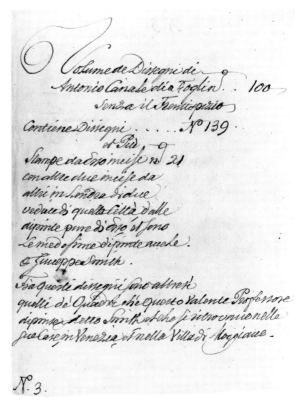

Description, in Smith's handwriting, of the contents of his volume containing drawings and etchings by Canaletto (Royal Library)

# Books

Books, whether manuscript or printed, were probably Smith's first love as a collector, and may even have been responsible for introducing him to the world of fine art. His first recorded book purchases date from the 1710s and in 1720 Smith issued the first of four printed lists of books. Each of these lists was produced principally with the intention of attracting a buyer. The first list consisted of 121 manuscripts; the entire collection was purchased by the Earl of Sunderland for £1,500. A further 101 manuscripts (also listed) were available through Smith's brother, John, in London late in 1722 but may have been sent back to Italy for sale. Two years later a catalogue of 227 early printed books belonging to Smith was issued; it reappeared in a second edition in 1737, with 21 additional titles. The fourth of Smith's catalogues was that which concerns us most: the *Bibliotheca Smithiana* issued (by the Pasquali Press) in 1755, which includes all the books in the Consul's library in 1751. The books listed therein were all transferred to the King in 1762. Indeed, the King's Librarian, Richard Dalton, checked the books off against the entries in the published catalogue before inscribing,

signing and dating two copies of his receipt, in Venice, on 28 January 1763.

The *Bibliotheca* – consisting of 519 pages of catalogue with an additional 66 pages of Addenda and Corrigenda – included all the incunabula listed in 1724, with around 30 additional early books. Morrison's recent analysis of Smith's books has highlighted both the high and the low points of his collection: the fine sixteenth- and seventeeth-century editions of the classics and of works relating to all branches of Italian culture, the complete reference collection of bibliography, and the large number of eighteenth-century books, including many in English. Smith is now recognised as one of the first collectors to take a serious

FACING PAGE

Five volumes from Smith's library: (above) the facsimile edition of Palladio's *Quattro Libri* produced by the Pasquali Press in 1768 (81); Giannone's History of Naples, 1742 (90); the volume containing engravings and drawings by Visentini (80); and (below) the volumes of drawings by Sebastiano Ricci and etchings by Marco Ricci

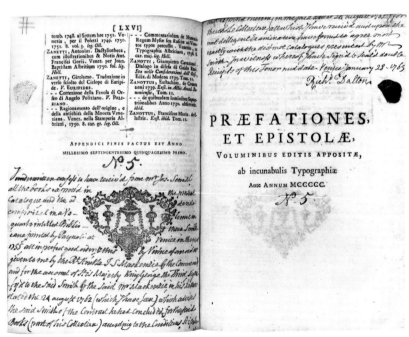

The receipt, signed by the King's Librarian, Richard Dalton, on 28 January 1763, for Smith's library, as listed in the *Bibliotheca Smithiana* (British Library, London)

Pages from two of Smith's illuminated manuscripts which passed to the British Museum in 1828 (with other books in the King's Library): the title page of Virgil's *Georgics* (left: BL, Kings MS 24, f.17) and the opening page of Cicero's *Orationes* (right: BL, Kings MS 19, f.11), with illuminations attributed to Bartolommeo Sanvito and to Gaspero da Verona

interest in incunabula. The fact that he was also a bookseller and publisher should not diminish our respect for his serious bibliographic interest and knowledge.

Most of the books issued by the Pasquali Press before 1752 were listed in the *Bibliotheca*. The Press, founded in the early 1730s, was named after Giovanni Battista Pasquali, a young classical scholar who acted as Smith's literary collaborator. But the Press was financed, controlled and directed by Smith himself and the Consul's artistic factotum, Visentini, acted as its principal designer. Attached to the Press was a bookshop called the 'Felicità delle Lettere' near the Rialto, which sold both Italian and imported books. Through these ventures Smith was

closely associated with the literary life of Venice, and indeed of all Europe. It was entirely appropriate that Goldoni's play 'Il Filosofo Inglese', first performed in 1754, in Venice, should have been dedicated to Smith.

Just as the pictures sold by Smith to George III were all in fine condition and newly framed, so Smith's books were also protected and adorned by fine bindings – of vellum or leather – as noted at the end of the basic bibliographic description in the *Bibliotheca*. A gilt impression of Smith's

FACING PAGE
The title pages of four books published by the Pasquali Press (84, 85, Guicciardini's History, and 86)

# P. VIRGILII MARONIS
# OPERA,
cum integris commentariis
## SERVII, PHILARGYRII, PIERII.
### ACCEDUNT
## SCALIGERI ET LINDENBROGII
Notae ad
## CULICEM, CIRIN, CATALECTA.
Ad Cod. MS. Regium Parisiensem recensuit
## PANCRATIUS MASVICIUS.
Cum indicibus absolutissimis.
### TOM. I.

## VENETIIS,
Excudit Jo. BAPTISTA PASCHALIUS.
ↀↀccxxxvi.
*SUPERIORUM PERMISSU, & PRIVILEGIO.*

---

# ANNALI D'ITALIA
## DAL PRINCIPIO
## DELL'ERA VOLGARE
SINO ALL'ANNO 1500.
### COMPILATI
## DA LODOVICO ANTONIO
MURATORI
Bibliotecario del SERENISSIMO
## DUCA DI MODENA.
### TOMO PRIMO
Dall'Anno primo dell'ERA volgare fino all'Anno 221.

## IN MILANO,
MDCCXLIV.
A spese di GIOVAMBATISTA PASQUALI
LIBRARO IN VENEZIA.

---

## DELLA
# ISTORIA
# D'ITALIA
## DI M. FRANCESCO
# GUICCIARDINI
### GENTILUOMO FIORENTINO
LIBRI XX.

### TOMO SECONDO.

## IN VENEZIA
Presso GIAMBATISTA PASQUALI
MDCCXXXVIII.
*CON LICENZA DE' SUPERIORI.*

---

### DESCRIZIONE
## DE' CARTONI DISEGNATI DA
## CARLO CIGNANI,
E DE' QUADRI DIPINTI DA
## SEBASTIANO RICCI
POSSEDUTI DAL SIGNOR
# GIUSEPPE SMITH
CONSOLE DELLA GRAN BRETAGNA
Appresso la Sereniss. REPUBBLICA di Venezia,
CON UN COMPENDIO DELLE VITE
DEI DUE CELEBRI PROFESSORI.

## IN VENEZIA,
MDCCXLIX.
Presso GIAMBATISTA PASQUALI.
*CON LICENZA DE' SUPERIORI.*

Giulio Clovio,
Composite illuminated sheet,
c1530 (**68**)

Arms is still to be found on both the front and back covers of many of his books. His concern for the appearance of books is clear from the specification in his will that copies of three books (including the *Dactyliotheca*) then proceeding through the Press should be presented, 'bound in red morocco leather gilt and with my coat of arms impressed on their covers' to various named individuals.

Until recently it was thought that – with the exception of a few 'art' books and volumes of drawings – the entire contents of the *Bibliotheca* was transferred, with the rest of George III's library, to the British Museum in 1828. However, it is now realised that this transfer involved only those books in the principal library at Buckingham House. Although the majority of Smith's books (and all his fine illuminated manuscripts) were indeed to be found in London, others were kept in the King's library at Cumberland (or 'Windsor') Lodge and were thus retained to form the basis of the new Royal Library (developed successively from the reign of George IV), which survives to this day at Windsor.

Smith's fine collection of 34 manuscripts (also included in the *Bibliotheca*) was an important part of George IV's gift to the nation and is now housed in the Department of Western Manuscripts of the British Library. The only one of Smith's illuminated manuscripts to survive at Windsor is the composite sheet of Missal illuminations by Clovio, noted in the Italian List alongside Smith's oil paintings, and presumably therefore framed up at the time.

Although the contents of the *Bibliotheca* had been purchased outright for the King in 1762, by the time of Smith's death in 1770 he had already accumulated a second – and almost equally important – collection of around 2,000 books. These were evidently acquired – 'recuperato' or recovered, as Smith put it – from 1752 onwards (there are no books published after 1751 in the *Bibliotheca*) and are included in various lists, one made by Smith himself and others made by those listing the contents of his home immediately after his death, or responsible for selling his effects. The books from Smith's 'second' library are also identifiable from the bookplates (designed by Visentini) which were applied to them. These exist in several different variants. Some name Smith as 'British Consul at Venice' (and must therefore date from 1744–60, or 1766), while others omit the official designation. No bookplate has yet been found in any book from Smith's 'first' library, as listed in the *Bibliotheca Smithiana*.

Visentini's illuminated title page to Smith's album of drawings by Giovanni Ambrogio Figino (**77**)

# Gems, coins and medals

The collection of cameos and intaglios which Smith sold to George III was illustrated (in engravings by G. B. Brustolon after drawings by A. M. Zanetti) and described (by A. F. Gori) in the *Dactyliotheca Smithiana*. Work on this publication was under way by 1753 and it was partly printed when Smith made his will in 1761. After the completion of the royal sale in 1762, it was only natural that the *Dactyliotheca* should appear – in 1767 – with a dedication to the King. Of the gems shown in the one hundred plates in that publication, 66 are identifiable in the Royal Collection.

Gori discussed Smith's gems chiefly in terms of their subject-matter, and rarely passed judgment about date or attribution: indeed he may never have seen the original stones. Current opinion suggests that although the majority of Smith's cameos are Italian works of the seventeenth and eighteenth centuries, there are also a few earlier ones, including a late imperial fragment of Zeus, carved from oriental onyx of three strata. The small group of intaglios are all thought to be early eighteenth century, fine and faithful copies of antique prototypes.

Smith's 'jewels, gold coins, cameos and intaglios, which by my books appear to have been purchased . . . as occasions have presented in a course of many years' were in 1761 on deposit with Santino Cambiaso, as surety against a debt of 16,000 ducats. Smith was particularly anxious that his 'Gemms' should be acquired by the King – as indeed they were. Like Smith's paintings, books and drawings, most of his gems are in uniform eighteenth-century mounts. Although Smith may well have placed the gems in these mounts prior to their sale, the mounts are apparently of English manufacture. Apart from the 16 lots of gems and jewels sold after Mrs Smith's death, no 'second collection' seems to have been accumulated.

The situation concerning coins and medals is less clear. Although it is fair to assume that the gold coins (specified as 'ancient Imperial') on deposit with Cambiaso in 1761 passed – with the gems – to George III (coins are indeed shown in the frontispiece to the *Dactyliotheca*), nothing can be proved in the absence of any precise list associated with the sale. George III's coin and medal collection, consisting of 4,082 'ancient coins' (including 575 gold pieces of the Imperial epoch) and 7,680 modern coins, totalling nearly 12,000, was transferred to the British Museum with the King's Library in 1828. Meanwhile, in 1777 William Hunter had purchased a (? second) collection of coins from the Consul's widow for £507.12s. This is now part of the Hunterian Museum in Glasgow.

The frontispiece of A. F. Gori's catalogue of Smith's collection of engraved gems (*Dactyliotheca Smithiana*, 1767). The central oval contains a portrait of King George III, to whom the collection had been sold in 1762

FACING PAGE
A selection of Smith's gems (83 and 88)

c

b

B. LICINIO.

a

# Smith's picture frames

## by Pippa Mason

A remarkable number of Consul Smith's paintings in the Royal Collection have remained in the eighteenth-century Venetian frames chosen by him. Few collections formed in Venice in the eighteenth century have remained intact and in most cases, where they have been broken up and dispersed, the frames have been changed by subsequent owners. The Royal Collection thus provides unique evidence about eighteenth-century Venetian frames. Those Smith frames that were replaced, adapted or added to, likewise provide clear indications of the changing taste in framing at the end of the eighteenth and beginning of the nineteenth centuries in England.

The most striking feature of the frames from the Consul Smith collection is the great homogeneity of frame types. Indeed the frames serve to identify pictures which belonged to Smith or were supplied by him to clients. It was clearly his practice to offer a framing service when supplying pictures, as indicated by his letter to Lord Essex of August 1733: 'I did my Self the Honour to write to my Lady Essex this day fortnight, to lett her know her two Pictures were finished . . . and withal I desir'd to know her Ladys Pleasure whether she would have them in Frames or not . . . The pictures with Gilt frames and charges will cost chequeens 52: 18/22 makes £27.8.11 sterling and without the frames chequeens 45 or £23.16.8'. A month later he wrote to Lady Essex: 'As soon as I received your Ladyships Commands I gave order for making the Frames for the two Pictures and they will be finished in a few days'.

The majority of Smith's frames are of a Venetian 'panel' type, characterised by an elegant rococo moulding with carved leaf, flower and 'C' scroll ornament, alternating with uncarved 'panels' (from which it derives its name). The pattern is typically Venetian and was widely used during the rococo period for both pictures and mirrors. Consul Smith used such frames not only for his contemporary Venetian pictures but also for the earlier Italian and Northern School paintings. No distinction was made for subject-matter; portraits, landscapes, religious and mythological subjects were all framed similarly. This was not unusual in the eighteenth century when frames were regarded very much as furniture and related more closely to the decorative scheme where they hung, than to the paintings they contained.

There are three distinct variations of Venetian 'panel' frames to be found in Smith's collection. The largest and most important group is highly distinctive in terms of the quality of the carving and the detail of its ornament [illustration a]. The motifs of scrolling leaves, flowers and 'C' scrolls, with a small dentil on the sight or back edge, are small in scale with only minor variations from frame to frame in order to accommodate the different sizes of paintings. The carving is unusually fine and sharp, accentuated by thinly-applied gesso, although in many cases the original crispness has been masked by layers of later regilding. Their uniform appearance must surely be the product of a single frame-maker. Unfortunately, the absence of surviving documents relating to Smith's personal expenditure means that we are unlikely to discover the identity of his frame-maker.

Precise dating of these frames is difficult. They can be found around pictures which entered Smith's collection in the 1720s, as well as those which Smith purchased from the Sagredo family in 1752. It is possible that this model was made continuously throughout this period, but it is more probable that Smith decided at a certain point to re-frame his collection and adopted this particular pattern to achieve a harmonious hanging scheme. This may have occurred during the 1740s and early 1750s when he was furnishing and decorating his palazzo at SS Apostoli.

The second variation of the Venetian 'panel' frame can be seen around the series of six large paintings by Sebastiano Ricci of scenes from the New Testament. Compared with the refined, rococo carving of Consul Smith's frame-maker, the ornament of these frames is more robust, harking back to a baroque tradition of carving, and suggesting a date in the 1720s contemporary with the paintings [illustration b]. Although these frames

FACING PAGE

a. Detail of a Venetian 'panel' frame, c1740–50: the frame pattern chosen by Smith for most pictures in his collection

b. Detail of a Venetian 'panel' frame, c1720–30: the pattern found around the series of New Testament paintings by Sebastiano Ricci

c. Detail of a Venetian 'panel' frame, c1717–30: a type found around gouaches by Marco Ricci

g. View of the Grand Corridor, Windsor Castle, showing several of Smith's frames with additions of 1828 (watercolour by Joseph Nash, RL 19782)

have clearly been cut through the moulding at the centres – usually a sign that a frame has been adapted and, therefore, is not original to the picture – there is no good reason to doubt that they were made for the pictures that they still surround. The cut may simply have been made to facilitate transport or get them through a small doorway. In the nineteenth century a small addition was made to the back edge of some of these frames in order to increase the width of the moulding.

The third category of Venetian 'panel' frames is a group, with slight variations to the pattern, around gouaches by Marco Ricci. They are more broadly carved and thickly gessoed, giving a soft appearance typical of Venetian frames of this period [illustration c]. A number retain their original eighteenth-century glasses. They are probably contemporary with the gouaches, which date from c1717–30, and therefore predate the frames made by Consul Smith's frame-maker.

Another Venetian frame pattern, which would appear to be unique to Consul Smith, is that around a series of twelve views of the Grand Canal by Canaletto in the Royal Collection. It is made from a narrow rococo moulding with carved ornament of repeating 'C' scrolls, acanthus leaves in the corners and a small rope twist on the back

edge. Other almost identical frames survive around Canalettos supplied by Smith to English clients; the series of twenty-two views of the Grand Canal, made for John, 4th Duke of Bedford, now at Woburn, and five pictures, formerly part of the Harvey series [illustration d]. They are also to be seen around the series of nineteen reduced versions, in *grisaille*, of allegorical tombs of illustrious Englishmen, commissioned by Owen McSwiney when he was in Venice. Although the precise nature of McSwiney's relationship with Smith is not clear, they would appear to have shared the same frame-maker. This frame pattern can be dated to the period of the production of these paintings between 1730 and 1735. All the frames of this type in the Royal Collection were given additions in the nineteenth century: the illustrated example belongs to a picture from the Harvey series.

FACING PAGE

d. Detail of a Venetian frame, with repeating 'C' scroll ornament, c1730–35 (Private Collection, New York)

e. Detail of an English 'Carlo Maratta' frame, c1760–80

f. Detail of an English 'Carlo Maratta' frame, with additions made in 1828 for George IV

ALESSANDRO TURCHI VALOUR

e

d

f

Of Smith's pictures no longer in Venetian frames, there is a large and significant group in matching English eighteenth-century 'Carlo Maratta' frames. This pattern of frame derived from a Roman prototype and was fashionable in England in the second half of the eighteenth century [illustration e]. One reason for the reframing of these pictures is suggested by a study of the arrangement of pictures in George III's palaces. Shortly after the arrival of Consul Smith's pictures in 1763, some of them were hung on the first floor at Buckingham House and can be seen – in their Venetian frames – in the background of Zoffany's painting of Queen Charlotte and her two eldest sons, painted about 1765. However, after Williams Chambers had completed his remodelling of Buckingham House in 1773, George III undertook a general re-arrangement of his pictures which resulted in the transfer of many of Smith's pictures to Kew. But an inventory of c1792 indicates that a group of Smith's larger Venetian pictures, including works by Canaletto, Visentini and Zuccarelli, were at the time hanging in the Hall at Buckingham House. These are precisely the pictures which are now in 'Carlo Maratta' frames. They may therefore have been reframed in order to harmonise with Chambers' neo-classical interior scheme. (It is also possible that some of these pictures arrived in England unframed, having formerly been set into the panelling of one of Smith's houses in Italy.)

In many cases the appearance of the Venetian and English eighteenth-century frames has been radically altered by additions made in the nineteenth century. In 1828 George IV moved a number of Smith's pictures to Windsor and their frames were remodelled in order to be incorporated into Wyatville's new decorative scheme for the Grand Corridor. The carver and gilder, Joseph Crouzet, was employed to enlarge the frames and to apply centre and corner ornaments [illustration f]. The elegant eighteenth-century frames were completely dwarfed by the new additions, but a watercolour by Joseph Nash of the Grand Corridor in 1846 [illustration g], showing a number of Smith's pictures hanging in their newly-embellished frames, demonstrates that it was necessary for the frames to be enlarged in order to hold their own alongside the new and massively wide frames made by George Morant for other pictures in the Corridor.

# Bibliography

For Smith see F. Haskell, *Patrons and Painters*, London, 1963 (new edn 1980), and F. Vivian, *Il Console Smith, Mercante e Collezionista*, Vicenza, 1971, *The Consul Smith Collection: Masterpieces of Italian Drawing from the Royal Library, Windsor Castle* (exh. cat.), Munich, 1989, and 'The last months of the life of Joseph Smith', *Apollo*, CXXXI, No.339, 1990, pp.309–12. A transcription of Smith's will and other important information is included in K. T. Parker, *The Drawings of Antonio Canaletto in the Collection of His Majesty The King at Windsor Castle*, London, 1948 (abbreviated as 'P'). The posthumous inventory of Smith's Venetian palace is transcribed in *Capricci Veneziani del Settecento* (exh. cat., ed. D. Succi), Castello di Gorizia, 1988, pp.515–50.

The Italian List was first published in L. Cust, 'Notes on pictures in the Royal Collection', *Burlington Magazine*, XXIII, 1913, pp.153ff, and the Flemish and Dutch List in A. Blunt and E. Croft-Murray, *Venetian Drawings of the XVII and XVIII Centuries in the Collection of Her Majesty The Queen at Windsor Castle*, London, 1957 (abbreviated as 'BV' and 'EC-M'), pp.19–23. The Lists are discussed (in Italian translation) in Vivian, *op. cit.*, 1971, pp.173–211.

Smith's Italian paintings are included in J. Shearman, *The Early Italian Pictures in the Collection of Her Majesty The Queen*, Cambridge, 1983 (abbreviated as 's') and (particularly) M. Levey, *The Later Italian Pictures in the Collection of Her Majesty The Queen*, London, 1964 (new edn, 1991; abbreviated as 'ML'). The few recognisable northern pictures are included in C. White, *The Dutch Pictures in the Collection of Her Majesty The Queen*, London, 1982 (abbreviated as 'CW') and in O. Millar, *The Tudor, Stuart and Early Georgian Pictures in the Collection of Her Majesty The Queen*, London, 1964 (abbreviated as 'OM'). The catalogue of the later Flemish pictures is in preparation.

Apart from the catalogues by Blunt and Parker mentioned above, drawings from Smith's collection are discussed in A. Blunt, *The Drawings of G. B. Castiglione and Stefano della Bella in the Collection of Her Majesty The Queen at Windsor Castle*, London, 1954 (abbreviated as 'BC'), O. Kurz, *Bolognese Drawings of the XVII and XVIII Centuries in the Collection of Her Majesty The Queen at Windsor Castle*, London, 1955 (abbreviated as 'K'), and A. E. Popham and J. Wilde, *The Italian Drawings of the XV and XVI Centuries in the Collection of His Majesty The King at Windsor Castle*, London, 1949 (reprinted, 1985; abbreviated as 'PW'). Facsimile reproductions of a selection of the Windsor Canaletto drawings were the subject of C. Miller, *Fifty Drawings by Canaletto from the Royal Library, Windsor Castle*, London and New York, 1983. Smith's print collection is discussed in an article by Antony Griffiths in *Print Quarterly*, VIII, no.2, June 1991 (pp.127–39). His library is best seen through the published catalogues, particularly the *Bibliotheca Smithiana* (1755), the *Catalogo di Libri* (1771) and the catalogue of the London sale (25 January 1773, Baker and Leigh). See also Stuart L. Morrison, 'Records of a Bibliophile. The Catalogues of Consul Joseph Smith and some aspects of his collecting', forthcoming in *The Book Collector*. Smith's manuscripts in the King's Library are discussed in G. F. Warner and J. P. Gilson, *British Museum: Catalogue of Western Manuscripts in the Old Royal and King's Collections*, III, London, 1921.

The gems will be included in the catalogue of gems and jewels in the Royal Collection (in preparation) and were discussed by Kirsten Aschengreen Piacenti in an article in *The Connoisseur*, June 1977, pp.79–83.

Many of the artists employed by Smith have been the subject of recent monographs. For Canaletto see particularly W. G. Constable, *Canaletto, Giovanni Antonio Canal*, 3rd edn, revised and amplified by J. G. Links, London, 1989, and *Canaletto. Paintings & Drawings* (exh. cat.), The Queen's Gallery, Buckingham Palace, London, 1980–81, which included the majority of his works in the Royal Collection. His etchings are discussed in R. Bromberg, *Canaletto's Etchings*, London, 1974 (abbreviated as 'Bromberg').

In general, there is a paucity of published material on the history of picture frames but a good source of information about Venetian frames is *Le Cornici Veneziane* by Giuseppe Morazzoni, Milan, c1940.

Otherwise it is necessary to turn to primary sources.
The correspondence between Smith and Lord and
Lady Essex is preserved in the British Library
(Add. MSS.27732). George III's hanging scheme at
Buckingham House is discussed in detail by Francis
Russell in 'King George III's picture hang at
Buckingham House', *Burlington Magazine*, CXXIX, 1987,
pp.524–531, and George IV's redecoration of Windsor
Castle is described by Geoffrey de Bellaigue and Pat
Kirkham in 'George IV and the Furnishing of Windsor
Castle', *Furniture History*, VIII, 1972, pp.1–34.

Joseph Smith's bookplate as British Consul (1744–60),
designed and engraved by Antonio Visentini

# Summary list of exhibits

**Sebastiano Ricci** (1659–1734)
1  Two heads (after Veronese), 1725–30
Canvas. 46.4 × 57.2 cms (ML 632)

**Antonio Visentini** (1688–1782)
2  Smith's villa at Mogliano: the entrance front, c1747
Pencil with grey wash. 23.3 × 27.3 cms (BV 538)

**Antonio Visentini** (1688–1782)
3  Smith's villa at Mogliano: the approach road, c1747
Pencil with grey wash. 23.2 × 27.3 cms (BV 541)

**Antonio Visentini** (1688–1782)
4  Title page with Smith's Arms, c1750
Pen and brown ink with watercolour and gold paint.
54.6 × 38.8 cms (BV 533)

**Antonio Visentini** (1688–1782)
5  Smith's villa at Mogliano: the garden front, c1747
Pencil with grey wash. 23.3 × 27.3 cms (BV 542)

**Antonio Visentini** (1688–1782)
6  Smith's villa at Mogliano: the garden, c1747
Pencil with grey wash. 23.3 × 27.3 cms (BV 539)

**Antonio Visentini** (1688–1782)
7  Designs for books
1) Pasquali's printer's mark, c1740
Pen and brown ink. 15 × 21.6 cms (BV 509)
2) The island of La Certosa, 1738
Pen and brown ink. 12.9 × 22.6 cms (BV 485)
3) Design for Ephraim Chambers's *Cyclopaedia*,
1748/9
Pen and brown ink. 9.3 × 16.3 cms (BV 549)

**Alessandro Turchi** (1578–1649)
8  Valour, c1610
Canvas. 131.4 × 60 cms (ML 660)

**Leandro Bassano** (1557–1622)
Portrait of a man with a statuette, c1592
Canvas. 87 × 66.7 cms. Signed (JS 29)

**School of Verona**
Portrait of an architect or scholar (possibly Daniele
Barbaro), c1540
Canvas. 101.9 × 82.8 cms (JS 326)

**Giovanni Bellini** (c1430–1516)
Portrait of a young man, c1507
Panel. 44 × 35.5 cms. Signed (JS 37)

**Bernardino Licinio** (c1485/90 – before 1549)
12  Portrait of an architect, 1541
Canvas. 99.7 × 82.5 cms. Signed and dated, with a
later identification as Palladio (JS 140)

**Canaletto** (1697–1768)
13  Rome: the Arch of Septimius Severus, 1742
Canvas. 180.3 × 105.7 cms. Signed and dated (ML 369)

**Canaletto** (1697–1768)
14  London: view from Somerset House to the City, c1750
Canvas. 108 × 188 cms (ML 374)

**Canaletto** (1697–1768)
15  Venice: the Grand Canal from the Carità to the
Bacino di S. Marco, c1730
Canvas. 47.9 × 80 cms (ML 386)

**Canaletto** (1697–1768)
16  Venice: the Grand Canal with S. Geremia and the
entrance to Cannaregio, c1730 and c1742
Canvas. 47 × 78.7 cms (ML 393)

**Canaletto** (1697–1768)
17  Venice: the Bacino di S. Marco on Ascension Day,
c1733–34
Canvas. 76.8 × 125.4 cms (ML 397)

**Canaletto** (1697–1768)
18  Venice: the Grand Canal from the Salute to the Riva,
c1731
Canvas. 47.6 × 80 cms (ML 388)

**Canaletto** (1697–1768)
19  Venice: the Grand Canal to the north of the Rialto,
c1730 and c1753
Canvas. 47.6 × 80 cms (ML 391)

**Canaletto** (1697–1768)
20  London: view from Somerset House to Westminster,
c1750
Canvas. 108 × 188.3 cms (ML 375)

**Canaletto** (1697–1768)
21  Rome: the Arch of Constantine, 1742
Canvas. 185.4 × 105.7 cms. Signed and dated (ML 370)

**Canaletto** (1697–1768)
22  Venice: the Piazzetta towards the Torre dell'Orologio,
c1727–29
Canvas. 172.1 × 134.9 cms (ML 381)

**Antonio Visentini (1688–1782) and
Francesco Zuccarelli (1702–88)**

23  Landscape with a triumphal arch to George II, 1746
Canvas. 81 × 131.4 cms. Signed and dated (ML 672)

**Sebastiano Ricci (1659–1734)**

24  The Adoration of the Magi, 1726
Canvas. 330.2 × 289.6 cms. Dated (ML 640)

**Marco (1676–1730)** and **Sebastiano Ricci**
(1659–1734)

25  Caprice with ruins, 1729
Canvas. 73 × 139.1 cms. Signed 'MR' and dated
(ML 628)

**Canaletto (1697–1768)**

26  Venice: Piazza S. Marco with the south-west corner
of the Basilica, c1727–29
Canvas. 172.7 × 134 cms (ML 380)

**Pietro Liberi (1614–87)**

27  Mythological subject, c1660
Canvas. 119 × 152 cms (ML 535)

**Sebastiano Ricci (1659–1734)**

28  Sacrifice of Polyxena, late 1720s
Canvas. 76.8 × 65.7 cms (ML 645)

**Bernardo Strozzi (1581–1644)**

29  Concert, 1630s
Canvas. 101.6 × 124.1 cms (ML 656)

**Sebastiano Ricci (1659–1734)**

30  The Holy Family with Saints Elizabeth and
John the Baptist, c1710
Canvas. 73 × 103.5 cms (ML 636)

**Pietro Liberi (1614–87)**

31  The Three Graces, 1670–80
Canvas. 120 × 152 cms (ML 536)

**Sebastiano Ricci (1659–1734)**

32  The Finding of Moses, 1720–30
Canvas. 71.1 × 62.5 cms (ML 647)

**Sir Anthony van Dyck (1599–1641)**

33  Zeger van Hontsum, c1630
Canvas. 108.6 × 84.5 cms (OM 155)

**Peeter Neeffs I (fl.1605, d.1656/1661) or
Peeter Neeffs II (1620 – after 1675)**

34  The interior of Antwerp Cathedral by night, c1640
Panel. 50.8 × 65.4 cms. Signed

**Frans Francken the Younger (1581–1642)**

35  A Cabinet, 1617
Panel. 76.5 × 119.1 cms. Signed and dated

**Johannes Vermeer (1632–75)**

36  A Lady at the Virginals, 1660–70
Canvas. 73.3 × 64.5 cms. Signed with monogram
(CW 230)

**Domenico Fetti (c1588–1623)**

37  Vincenzo Avogadro, 1620
Canvas. 114.6 × 90.2 cms (ML 470)

**Peeter Neeffs I (fl.1605, d.1656/1661) or
Peeter Neeffs II (1620 – after 1675)**

38  The interior of Antwerp Cathedral by day, c1640
Panel. 46 × 63.8 cms

**Jan Molenaer (1609/10–68)**

39  Head of a laughing youth, c1630
Panel. 48.9 × 38.4 cms (CW 116)

**Frans Post (c1612–80)**

40  Village in Brazil, 1650–60 (?)
Panel. 51.1 × 59.1 cms (CW 151)

**Canaletto (1697–1768)**

41  Venice: the interior of S. Marco by night (?), c1725
Canvas. 33 × 22.5 cms (ML 398)

**Canaletto (1697–1768)**

42  Venice: the interior of S. Marco by day, c1755
Canvas. 36.5 × 33.5 cms (ML 399)

**Canaletto (1697–1768)**

43  Venice: the Libreria and Campanile from the
Piazzetta, late 1730s
Pen and brown ink over pencil, with pin pointing.
27 × 37.5 cms (P 25)

**Canaletto (1697–1768)**

44  Venice: the Grand Canal from the Palazzo Corner to
the Palazzo Contarini degli Scrigni, c1734
Pen and brown ink over pencil, with pin pointing.
27 × 37.3 cms (P 17)

**Canaletto (1697–1768)**

45  Venice: the Libreria looking west, c1735
Pen and brown ink over pencil, with pin pointing.
18.8 × 27.6 cms (P 43)

**Canaletto (1697–1768)**

46  Venice: the Libreria looking west, c1735
Pen and brown ink with grey wash over pencil,
with pin pointing. 18.7 × 26.5 cms (P 44)

**Canaletto** (1697–1768)

47 Capriccio with terrace and loggia, c1760
Pen and ink and grey wash over pencil and stylus.
36.5 × 52.6 cms (P 141)

**Canaletto** (1697–1768)

48 Venice: Castello from the Motta di S. Antonio,
late 1730s
Pen and brown ink with grey wash over pencil.
15.5 × 34.4 cms (P 65)

**Canaletto** (1697–1768)

49 Venice: S. Elena and the distant coastline of the Lido,
late 1730s
Pen and brown ink with grey and brown wash.
15.8 × 34.8 cms (P 68)

**Canaletto** (1697–1768)

50 Venice: the water entrance of the Arsenal, late 1730s
Pen and brown ink over pencil, with pin pointing.
27.1 × 37.3 cms (P 29)

**Canaletto** (1697–1768)

51 Capriccio with the Arco dei Pantani and the Temple
of Mars Ultor in a fanciful setting, early 1740s
Pen and brown ink with grey wash over pencil,
stylus and pin pointing. 19.5 × 27.4 cms (P 112)

**Canaletto** (1697–1768)

52 Veduta ideata: the pavilion and courtyard of a villa,
late 1750s
Pen and brown ink with grey wash over pencil,
stylus and pin pointing. 21.6 × 33.6 cms (P 140)

**Canaletto** (1697–1768)

53 London: view from the terrace of Somerset House
to the City, c1750
Pen and brown ink with grey wash over pencil,
stylus and pin pointing. 20 × 48.4 cms (P 114)

**Canaletto** (1697–1768)

54 Venice: Piazza S. Marco with the south-west corner
of the Basilica, c1727
Pen and brown ink over traces of pencil.
23.3 × 18 cms (P 1)

**Canaletto** (1697–1768)

55 Venice: the Grand Canal with S. Geremia and the
entrance to Cannaregio, 1734
Pen and brown ink over pencil and pin pointing.
18.6 × 27 cms. Dated on verso (P 37)

**Canaletto** (1697–1768)

56 London: Westminster Bridge, c1750
Pen and brown ink with grey wash, over pencil and
pin pointing. 29.3 × 48.2 cms (P 118)

**Canaletto** (1697–1768)

57 Padua: distant view of S. Antonio, c1740
Pen and brown ink over pencil. 20 × 28.9 cms.
Signed on verso (P 74)

**Canaletto** (1697–1768)

58 Padua: bridge and houses on the Brenta canal, c1740
Pen and brown ink over traces of pencil and red chalk,
with pin pointing. 18.7 × 27.3 cms (P 88)

**Canaletto** (1697–1768)

59/1 Title plate, c1744
Etching (2nd state). Platemark 29.6 × 42.5 cms.
Signed (Bromberg 1)

**Canaletto** (1697–1768)

59/2 The portico with a lantern, c1743
Etching (3rd state). Platemark 30 × 43 cms.
Signed (Bromberg 10)

**Canaletto** (1697–1768)

59/3 The Procuratie Nuove and S. Geminiano, c1740
Etching (1st state). Platemark 14.3 × 21 cms.
Signed (Bromberg 25)

**Canaletto** (1697–1768)

59/4 Alpine landscape with church, houses and two pillars,
c1735
Etching (single state, unique impression). Platemark
14.3 × 20.9 cms (Bromberg 35)

**Sebastiano Ricci** (1659–1734)

60 The Adoration of the Magi, 1726
Pen and grey ink with grey wash. 33.2 × 31.2 cms
(BV 238)

**Sebastiano Ricci** (1659–1734)

61 Two heads for *The Adoration*, 1726
Black, white and coloured chalks on grey-blue paper.
28.8 × 41.8 cms (BV 250)

**Sebastiano Ricci** (1659–1734)

62 The Sacrifice of Polyxena, late 1720s
Pen and brown ink and brown wash over traces of
pencil. 20.3 × 28.3 cms (BV 270)

**Sebastiano Ricci** (1659–1734)

63 Woman carrying a child, c1727
Pen and brown ink with brown and grey wash over
pencil. 21.6 × 15.4 cms (BV 312)

**Sebastiano Ricci** (1659–1734)

64 The Communion of St Lucy, 1730
Pen and brown ink with grey wash over pencil.
28.5 × 20.2 cms (BV 282)

**Sebastiano Ricci** (1659–1734)

65 The Magdalen anointing Christ's feet, c1729/30
Pen and brown ink with grey wash. 24.5 × 34.8 cms
(BV 268)

**Sebastiano Ricci** (1659–1734)

66 Head of the Pharisee for *The Magdalen*, c1729/30
Black, white and red chalks. 31.2 × 24.4 cms (BV 269)

**Sebastiano Ricci** (1659–1734)

67 Design for a monument to Isaac Newton (1642–1727),
c1728
Pen and grey and brown ink with grey and brown
wash over pencil. 40.3 × 32.7 cms (BV 343)

**Giulio Clovio** (1498–1578)

68 Composite illuminated sheet, c1530
Tempera and gold paint, with some gold leaf. Vellum,
66.3 × 42.1 cms (PW 40–3)

**Zaccaria Valaresso** (1686–1769)

69 'Baiamonte Tiepolo. Poema eroicomico', 1751
Manuscript

**Giovanni Benedetto Castiglione** (c1610–63/5)

70 Nativity with God the Father, c1655
Drawn in oil paint. 39.5 × 54.7 cms (BC 131)

**Ludovico Carracci** (1555–1619)

71 Saints and angels in adoration c1605
Pen and ink with brown wash over black chalk with
white heightening on brown washed paper.
45.6 × 20.6 cms (W 46). Incorporating a drawing by
Parmigianino (1503–40) of a girl holding a crucifix

**Agostino Carracci** (1557–1602)

72 Pluto, 1592
Black chalk heightened with white on faded grey-
green paper. 25.3 × 28 cms (W 98)

**Giovanni Ambrogio Figino** (c1548/51–1608)

73 Laocöon, c1580
Black chalk on blue paper. 41.6 × 25.4 cms
(PW 326(52))

**Raphael** (1483–1520)

74 Massacre of the Innocents, c1510
Red chalk over stylus underdrawing and transferred
black chalk. 24.4 × 41.1 cms (PW 793)

**Guido Reni** (1575–1642)

75 Falling giant, c1637
Red chalk. 28.3 × 23.2 cms (K 364)

**Giovanni Benedetto Castiglione** (c1610–63/5)

76 Christ on the Cross with angels and mourning figures,
c1660
Drawn in oil paint. 26.2 × 38.9 cms (BC 192)

**Antonio Visentini** (1688–1782)

77 Title page to volume of drawings by Giovanni
Ambrogio Figino, c1750
Pen and brown ink with watercolour, bodycolour and
gold paint. Signed (BV 536)

78 **Bibliotheca Smithiana** (Venice: G. B. Pasquali,
1755)

**Joseph Smith** (c1674–1770)

79 List of contents of Visentini volume, c1750
Manuscript

80 Volume of drawings and prints by Antonio Visentini
(1688–1782) bound for Smith, c1750 (147/4)

**Andrea Palladio** (1518–80)

81 *I Quattro Libri dell' Architettura*
('Venice: Dominico de' Franceschi, 1570': facsimile
edition, published Venice: G. B. Pasquali, 1768)

**Anton Francesco Gori** (1691–1757)

82 *Dactyliotheca Smithiana* (Venice: G. B. Pasquali,
1767), I

83 Head of Zeus. Probably late Hellenistic, 2nd/1st
century BC.
Onyx cameo, carved in three strata. 6.4 × 5.1 cms
(Gem VII/215)

**Virgil** (70–19 BC)

84 *Opere* (Venice: G. B. Pasquali, 1736), I

**Ludovico Antonio Muratori** (1672–1750)

85 *Annali d' Italia* (Milan: G. B. Pasquali, 1744), I

**Pietr' Ercole Gherardi**

86 *Descrizione de' cartoni disegnati da Carlo Cignani
e de' quadri dipinti da Sebastiano Ricci* (Venice:
G. B. Pasquali, 1749)

**Carlo Goldoni** (1707–93)

87 *Opere* (Venice: G. B. Pasquali, 1761), IV

88 Smith's collection of cameos and intaglios. Italian,
sixteenth to eighteenth centuries.

**Edward Wright**

89 *Some observations made in travelling through France, Italy, &c* (London: T. Ward and E. Wicksteed, 1730)

**Pietro Giannone** (1676–1748)

90 *Histoire civile du royaume de Naples* (The Hague: P. Gosse and I. Beauregard, 1742), II

**André Morell** (1646–1703)

91 *Thesaurus Morellianus* (Amsterdam: J. Wetstenium and W. Smith, 1734), I

**Joannes Gratianus**

92 *Historiarum Venetarum* (Padua: J. Manfrè, 1728), I and II

**Luigi Ferdinando Marsigli** (1658–1730)

3 *Danubius Pannonico-mysicus* (The Hague: P. Gosse, R.C. Alberts, P. De Hondt, and Amsterdam: H. Uytwerf, F. Changuion, 1726) V

**Francesco Bartolozzi** (1728–1815) **after Francesco Zuccarelli** (1702–88)

4 'Da l'esca un picciol rivo a sobria mensa', c1762 Engraving. 35.3 × 45.6 cms (Calabi & De Vesme 2447)

**Francesco Zuccarelli** (1702–88)

5 Landscape with a woman fording a stream, c1744 Canvas. 36.8 × 50.2 cms (ML 701)

**Antonio Visentini** (1688–1782)

6 Title page of the *Prospectus Magni Canalis Venetiarum*, 1735 Engraving. 27.1 × 42.7 cms

**Marco Ricci** (1676–1730)

7 Hall with staircase, c1726 Pen and brown ink with brown wash over pencil. 29.3 × 28.4 cms (BV 169)

**Marco Ricci** (1676–1730)

8 Farinelli in walking dress, c1729/30 Pen and brown ink over pencil. 31.8 × 11.8 cms (ECM 72)

**Marco Ricci** (1676–1730)

Senesino and Faustina, 1728/29 Pen and brown ink over pencil. 18.4 × 24.5 cms. Dated *1728* (ECM 67)

**Marco Ricci** (1676–1730)

Landscape with a rustic bridge, c1719 Pen and brown ink and brown wash. 37.1 × 53.8 cms. Signed in monogram (BV 82)

**Marco Ricci** (1676–1730)

101 Travellers on a rocky track, c1725 Pen and brown ink over traces of pencil. 25.1 × 36.1 cms (BV 86)

**Marco Ricci** (1676–1730)

102 Herds terrified by a storm, c1727 Pen and brown ink with brown wash heightened with bodycolour, on blue-grey paper. 38.8 × 52.8 cms (BV 157)

**Giovanni Battista Piazzetta** (1683–1754)

103 Self-portrait, c1730 Black and white chalks on grey-brown paper. 39.4 × 29.4 cms (BV 29)

**Rosalba Carriera** (1675–1757)

104 Self-portrait, c1745 Pastel on paper. 57.2 × 47 cms (ML 446)

**Marco Ricci** (1676–1730)

105 Italian town caprice, 1717/19 Bodycolour on leather. 33 × 45.7 cms (ML 598)

**Marco Ricci** (1676–1730)

106 Woodland scene with bandits, c1725 Bodycolour on leather. 30.5 × 45.7 cms (ML 613)

**Marco Ricci** (1676–1730)

107 Allegory with a monument to Isaac Newton (1642–1727), 1728 Bodycolour on leather. 31.8 × 45.1 cms. Dated (ML 616)

**Style of Gonzales Coques** (1614/18–84)

108 Portrait of a man, c1655–60 Copper. 30.5 × 21.1 cms

**Francesco Zuccarelli** (1702–88)

109 Landscape with Diana and the chase, c1740 Copper. 53.3 × 40 cms (ML 678)

**Style of Gonzales Coques** (1614/18–84)

110 Portrait of a man holding gloves, c1655–60 Copper. 30.3 × 22.2 cms

**Marco Ricci** (1676–1730)

111 Landscape with a storm, c1727 Bodycolour on leather. 31.1 × 45.7 cms (ML 617)

**Marco Ricci** (1676–1730)

112 Courtyard of a villa, c1728 Bodycolour on leather. 31.1 × 45.7 cms (ML 593)

**Marco Ricci** (1676–1730)

113 The outskirts of a town with women washing linen, c1720
Bodycolour on leather. 32.1 × 45.7 cms (ML 619)

**Pietro Longhi** (1702?–85)

114 Blind man's buff, 1744
Panel. 48.3 × 58.4 cms. Dated 174[4] (ML 538)

# Index

46545 A

Designed by Graham Johnson
Printed by Balding + Mansell plc